■SCHOLASTIC

BEST PRACTICES in Action

Fluency Practice
Read-Aloud Plays

GRADES 3–4

BY KATHLEEN M. HOLLENBECK

NEW YORK • TORONTO • LONDON • AUCKLAND • SYDNEY
MEXICO CITY • NEW DELHI • HONG KONG • BUENOS AIRES

Teaching *Resources*

To the patient

and dedicated teachers

who guide

and encourage students

on the path toward fluency.

Cover design by Brian LaRossa
Interior design by Kathy Massaro
Interior art by Delana Bettoli, Michelle Dorenkamp, Mike Gordon, Mike Moran, and Bari Weissman

ISBN–13: 978-0-439-55420-6
ISBN–10: 0-439-55420-9

1 2 3 4 5 6 7 8 9 10   40   14 13 12 11 10 09 08 07 06

Contents

INTRODUCTION

*f*luency, the ability to decode words quickly and accurately, is more than just a buzzword in education. It is a fundamental skill that must be achieved in order for readers to find meaning in words.

Oral reading offers tremendous insight into a student's level of fluency. The fluent reader glides through text almost effortlessly, reading with meaning, expression, and appropriate pacing. A struggling reader labors over words, deciphering them in a slow, halting manner that hinders comprehension.

Training and practice are essential to achieving reading fluency, and oral reading offers an unmatched opportunity for both. *Read-Aloud Plays for Building Fluency: Grades 3–4* includes 14 oral reading opportunities that make reading practice easy, entertaining, and rewarding. The plays explore topics from core-curricular areas and adhere to national standards for third and fourth grades.

In addition to the plays, inside this book you'll find activities to strengthen skills in fluency, phonics, and oral reading; a section devoted to enhancing the Readers Theater experience (see Using Readers Theater, page 14); and tools for assessment, including a teacher rubric and a checklist students can use to guide and monitor their own reading progress (see Assessing Fluency, page 8). The plays and activities target specific skills designed to increase word recognition, decoding accuracy, use of expression, and ultimately, comprehension— the primary goal of reading instruction.

The text of each play has been leveled using readability scores from the Lexile Framework for Reading (see chart, page 13). These scores offer guidelines to help you select the scripts that best match the needs and reading levels of each student. The plays are ready for use to practice, strengthen, and assess skills in reading fluency. And they all share the same objective: to give students practice reading comfortably, confidently, and with enthusiasm, helping to build an ever-growing flock of fluent readers within the walls of your classroom.

Fluency: An Overview

What Is Fluency?

Fluency is the mark of a proficient reader. When a student reads text quickly, gets most of the words right, and uses appropriate expression and phrasing, we say that he or she has achieved fluency. Fluency frees readers from the struggle that slows them down. Hence, they are able to read for meaning and to understand. They can attend to the details of text, pausing as indicated and varying tone and pace to enhance comprehension for both themselves and potential listeners.

How Does Fluency Develop?

As with every skill worth developing, fluency sharpens with experience. Exposure to print, immersion in a rich linguistic environment, and practice, practice, practice all lead to fluent reading.

From the emergent on up, readers must learn and apply tools to help them advance. The National Institute for Literacy (NIFL) speaks of fluency as a skill in flux.

> "Fluency is not a stage of development at which readers can read all words quickly and easily. Fluency changes, depending on what readers are reading, their familiarity with the words, and the amount of their practice with reading text. Even very skilled readers may read in a slow, labored manner when reading texts with many unfamiliar words or topics." (NIFL, 2001)

Readers are most comfortable (and most fluent) when reading what they have seen before or what they know most about. When venturing beyond these areas, they must rely on word attack skills, prior knowledge, and the host of tools that have helped them advance to this point.

Ways to Build Fluency

Two words encompass what readers require for the development of fluency: *exposure* and *practice*. To foster fluent reading using the plays in this book:

✳ **MODEL FLUENT READING.** Do an interactive read-aloud. As you read, model (and point out) aspects of fluent reading such as phrasing, pacing, and expression. Help students understand that people aren't born knowing how do this; they learn it by hearing it and trying it themselves. Also ask open-ended questions before, during, and after the reading,

> "Fluent readers read aloud effortlessly and with expression. Their reading sounds natural, as if they are speaking. Readers who have not yet developed fluency read slowly, word by word. Their oral reading is choppy and plodding."
>
> NATIONAL INSTITUTE FOR LITERACY, 2001

soliciting students' prior knowledge and extending their understanding, comprehension, and connection with the topic. This connection can advance student interaction with the text and promote optimal conditions for fluency.

✳ **PROVIDE STUDENTS WITH PLENTY OF READING PRACTICE.** Oral reading is highly effective for tracking and strengthening fluency. It enables both the reader and the listener to hear the reader and assess progress, and it allows the listener to provide guidance as needed. Encourage reading practice with any of the following:

● **Repeated Reading:** Read aloud while a student listens. Then read again while the student follows along. Finally, have the student read the same text aloud alone. This technique is most helpful for struggling readers.

● **Paired Repeated Reading:** Group students in pairs, matching above-level readers with on-level readers and on-level readers with those below level. Encourage partners to take turns reading aloud to each other, each reading a short passage three times and then getting feedback. This manner of grouping provides every struggling reader with a more proficient reader to model.

● **Readers Theater:** Students work in groups to rehearse and perform one or more plays from this book. See Using Readers Theater, page 14, for more.

✳ **SELECT APPROPRIATE TEXT.** To develop fluency, a student must practice reading text at his or her independent reading level—the level at which he or she is able to accurately decode 96 to 100 percent of the words in a given text. This level varies for every student. By assessing each student's reading level up front, you will be prepared to select appropriate texts and ensure that your students get a lot of practice reading at a level at which they achieve success (Rasinski, 2003; Worthy and Broaddus, 2001/2002). For information about how to use text to assess fluency, see Assessing Fluency, page 8.

✳ **GIVE ROOM TO GROW.** To help a student advance in fluency, present text at his or her instructional level. This text can be read with 90 to 95 percent accuracy. With a little help, the student can get almost all the words right (Blevins, 2001; Rasinski, 2003).

✳ **PROVIDE DIRECT INSTRUCTION AND FEEDBACK.** Prepare students before they read. First review phonics skills they will need to decode words. Draw attention to sight words, root words, affixes, and word chunks. Preteach difficult or unfamiliar words. Demonstrate the use of intonation, phrasing, and expression, and tell students when they have done these well. Listen to students read, and offer praise as well as helpful tips for the next attempt.

❋ **HIGHLIGHT PHRASING.**

One of the most effective ways to help students who are struggling with fluency is to use phrase-cued text. Phrase-cued text is marked by slashes to indicate where readers should pause. One slash indicates a pause or meaningful chunk of text within a sentence. Two slashes indicates a longer pause at the end of a sentence. Ready-made samples of phrase-cued text are available (see Resources for Reading Fluency, Comprehension, and Readers Theater, page 15), but you can also convert any passage of text to phrase-cued text by reading it aloud, listening for pauses and meaningful chunks of text, and drawing slashes in the appropriate places. (See the example, above, from the play "Railroad to Freedom," page 39.) Model fluent reading with proper phrasing and invite students to practice with the text you have marked.

> **Narrator 1:** Harriet/ leads the way/ through the woods.// The travelers/ step over logs,/ duck under tree limbs,/ and walk/ all night long.// In time,/ they come to/ a river.//
>
> **Harriet:** See that bridge?// When we cross it,/ crawl under the bushes/ and hide.// It's almost daylight,/ and slave hunters/ will be/ looking for us.// Stay hidden/ until night.

Where Does Vocabulary Fit In?

Stumbling over words constitutes one of the main setbacks on the way to fluency. It remains in your students' best interest, then, to grow familiar with words they will likely encounter in reading. Cunningham and Allington (2003) urge active use of word walls, inviting student participation in choosing words to put on the walls, eliminating words rarely used, and reviewing the list words daily.

Enhancing Comprehension

In all reading instruction, it is important to remember that reading imparts meaning, and so the fundamental goal of reading is to comprehend. All other instruction—phonics, phonemic awareness, auditory discrimination—is wasted effort if comprehension gets lost in the process. Consequently, those who find no purpose or meaning in the written word will soon lose interest in reading it altogether.

   Avoid this by teaching your students strategies to enhance comprehension. Help them learn to question the text they are reading. *What is the message? Does it make sense to them? Do they know what it means?* Find out by asking questions. Ask questions before students read, to prepare them for the play. Ask as they read, to deepen their understanding of the text. Ask additional questions after they read, to clear up any comprehension issues and summarize the play. Teach your students to formulate questions of their own to give them a vested interest in what they are reading.

> "As the child approaches a new text he is entitled to an introduction so that when he reads, the gist of the whole or partly revealed story can provide some guide for a fluent reading. He will understand what he reads if it refers to things he knows about, or has read about previously, so that he is familiar with the topic, the vocabulary or the story itself."
>
> (CLAY, 1991)

Assessing Fluency

There are two ways to assess a student's progress in fluency: informally and formally. Informal assessment involves listening to students read aloud, noting how easily, quickly, and accurately they read, and deciding how well they attend to phrasing, expression, and other elements. Formal assessment involves timing a student's oral reading to create a tangible record of his or her progress throughout the school year.

To conduct an informal assessment of students' reading fluency, use the reproducible Teacher Rubric for Oral Reading Fluency on page 9. Have a student read aloud for five to seven minutes while you note on the form the strategies the student uses as well as his or her reading strengths and difficulties.

Students can monitor their own progress using the Student Checklist for Self-Assessment on page 10. Photocopy and laminate this form for each student. Review the checklist components with students many times, until they understand the purpose of the checklist and the meaning of each statement. Encourage students to mentally complete the checklist from time to time to track their own reading fluency.

To carry out what is called timed repeated reading, select a passage of text (150–200 words) that is at the student's independent reading level and that he or she has never read before. Have the student read aloud the passage for one minute. Track your own copy of the text while he or she reads, marking words omitted or pronounced incorrectly. Count the number of words the student read correctly. Then give the student three one-minute opportunities (in separate sessions) to read the same text, and average the scores to obtain his or her oral reading fluency rate.*

In Conclusion

Does fluency instruction work? Research has shown that concentrated reading instruction can dramatically improve reading comprehension and fluency, which in turn affect academic performance, self-esteem, and overall achievement. With this in mind, it is not only helpful to instruct with an eye toward fluency, it is essential.

---

* For more detailed information on timed reading, consult Blevins (2001, pp. 9–12) and Rasinski (2003, pp. 82–83).

Teacher Rubric for Oral Reading Fluency

Child's Name: _____ Date: _____

Grade: _____ Passage: _____

> For each category, circle the number that best describes the student's performance.

Accuracy

4	Recognizes most words; works to pronounce unfamiliar words, repeating them to self-correct if necessary.
3	Recognizes most words; works to pronounce unfamiliar words, self-correcting if necessary; sometimes requires assistance.
2	Struggles to decode and decipher words; hesitates before attempting to pronounce new words; usually requires assistance.
1	Recognizes very few words; makes no attempt to pronounce unfamiliar words.

Expression and Volume

4	Uses expression and volume that is natural to conversational language and that varies according to the content of the text.
3	Uses expression and volume that is appropriate to conversational language and the content of the text; sometimes hesitates when unsure of text.
2	Often speaks softly and in a monotone; pays little attention to expression or volume; focuses on getting through the text.
1	Reads words in a monotone and in a quiet voice.

Phrasing

4	Groups words into meaningful phrases or chunks of text.
3	Usually groups words into meaningful phrases or chunks of text.
2	Reads primarily in groups of two or three words.
1	Reads word by word without meaning.

Pace

4	Reads at a suitable pace and responds to punctuation with appropriate pausing and intonation.
3	Usually reads at a suitable pace and attends to most punctuation with appropriate pausing and intonation; halts at times when unsure.
2	Reads slowly, sometimes two or three words at a time; halts often; pays little attention to punctuation or pacing.
1	Reads words slowly in a string; does not heed punctuation.

Prosody

4	Attends to the rhythm of language, reading comfortably and without hesitating or halting.
3	Occasionally halts or runs sentences together when challenged by words or sentence structure.
2	Reads smoothly at times but most often slowly.
1	Reading sounds stilted and unnatural and lacks meaning.

Source: Adapted from "Training Teachers to Attend to Their Students' Oral Reading Fluency," by J. Zutell and T. V. Rasinski, 1991, *Theory Into Practice*, 30, pp. 211–217. Used with permission of the authors.

Fluency Practice Read-Aloud Plays: Grades 3–4   Scholastic Teaching Resources

Name: _____

How Carefully Do I Read?

	Most of the Time	Sometimes	Hardly Ever
1 I say a word again if it does not sound right.	☐	☐	☐
2 I pay attention to punctuation at the end of a sentence.	☐	☐	☐
3 I try to read without stopping after every word.	☐	☐	☐
4 I read with expression.	☐	☐	☐
5 I am ready to speak when it is my turn.	☐	☐	☐

What I Need to Work on:

_____

_____

_____

_____

Adapted from *35 Rubrics & Checklists to Assess Reading and Writing* by Adele Fiderer. Permission to reuse granted by the author.
Fluency Practice Read-Aloud Plays: Grades 3–4   Scholastic Teaching Resources

Using the Plays to Enhance Fluency

A Fluency Mini-Lesson

Let this sample mini-lesson serve as a model for using the plays to strengthen and assess reading fluency. The mini-lesson may be conducted with small groups or with the class as a whole.

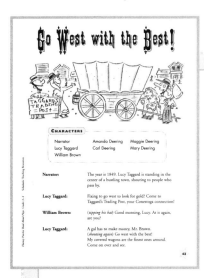

Go West with the Best!

PREPARATION: Give each student a copy of the play "Go West with the Best!" (pages 43–46). Note: For this model lesson, give students a copy of the same play. As they become more fluent, select different plays for each group to rehearse and perform.

Prereading

1. Introduce unfamiliar or difficult words students will come across in the text, such as *bustling*, *tongue*, and *stretch*, as well as some of the more complex high-use words: *family* and *next*. Help students decode the words. Review them several times to aid recognition and boost fluency. (See Preparing for Difficult or Unfamiliar Text, page 13, for more.)

2. Review reading techniques that promote fluency, such as reading from left to right, "smooshing" words together, and crossing the page with a steady, sweeping eye movement (Blevins, 2001).

3. Divide the class into small groups, equal in size to the number of characters in the play.

Reading and Modeling

1. Depending on students' level of reading proficiency, you may want to read the play aloud and then invite the group to read along with you. As you read, point out ways in which your pacing, intonation, and expression lend meaning to the text. You might ask:

   "Did you notice how my voice rose at the end of the sentence 'I wouldn't want Amanda and Carl to get stuck on the trail!'? That's what we do when we see an exclamation point. We know the sentence tells something exciting; we use our voices to make it sound that way."

2. Try reading the sentences without the inflection. Observe aloud that questions read without the appropriate tone sound flat and stilted, without depth, character, or expression.

3. Then point out other punctuation marks that require voice or tone changes, for example, on page 44, the question mark in *What's this piece of wood sticking out from the front?* and the period in *Nice wagon, Lucy.*

4. Read the play aloud again, inviting students to read aloud with you as they are able. Note: If you feel that a group of readers is already proficient, preview the words and then have students read the play aloud without modeling.

5. Once readers have read the play several times, go back and emphasize aspects of phonics and vocabulary that will increase their understanding of language, encourage appropriately paced, accurate reading, and deepen comprehension. "Go West with the Best!" presents opportunities to explore such topics as:

✳ **phrasing:** Readers must pause briefly after all commas. They will pause for a longer time after a comma that joins two sentences (*The wagon stays dry, and so do you!*) than after a comma that is preceded by a transitional word or phrase, such as *Well, I might just have some business for you*, or *Amanda, this wagon will hold you, your family, and everything you want to take west.*

✳ **use of ellipses:** An ellipsis indicates the need for a pause between words. Have students identify the places where ellipses are used in this play, such as on page 46 where we find: *Except...how much do your wagons cost, Lucy?* and *Any one of mine will take you out west...and back if you start feeling homesick!* Talk about times in real life when people pause in casual conversation, allowing their voices to trail off within or at the end of a sentence. Help students make the connection between the visual use of ellipses in written dialogue and the oral pause used in speech.

✳ **consonant combinations:** Draw attention to consonant blends and digraphs, such as the initial consonant blend *str* in *stretch* (a word which also ends with the digraph *ch*). Also point out the word *clothes*, which begins with a blend and contains a digraph in the middle. Extend the learning by brainstorming additional words that contain the same consonant blends or digraphs or a different combination.

✳ **vernacular:** The dialect of a place or time period can serve as a powerful tool in conveying the flavor of a tale. Have students locate and experiment with examples of this kind of dialogue in "Go West with the Best!" For example, on page 44, Amanda Deering says, *My husband and I are fixing to take the girls out west next month....* Also, on page 45, Lucy Taggard says, *Not one lick of water soaks through.*

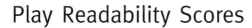

Play Readability Scores

The chart below shows the readability scores of the plays in this collection. The texts were leveled using the Lexile Framework for Reading. These scores offer guidelines to help you select the plays that best match the needs and reading levels of each student. For more information about the Lexile Framework, go to www.lexile.com. (See Preparing for Difficult or Unfamiliar Text, below, for more.)

	Play Title	Lexile Score*
1.	Coyote and the Rock	350L
2.	The Missing Trophy	380L
3.	The Wolf and the Seven Young Kids	390L
4.	Meeting Thomas Edison	400L
5.	Midnight at Old Truman's	410L
6.	Railroad to Freedom	430L
7.	Go West with the Best!	470L
8.	The Bremen Town Musicians	500L
9.	Heroine on the Titanic	550L
10.	Lucky Hans	560L
11.	Remembering Uncle Freemont	600L
12.	About Ten Bowls of Porridge	610L
13.	The Selfish Girl	650L
14.	Earthquake!	700L

* The Lexile score is based on dialogue text only. Conventional play formatting (such as the names that indicate which character is speaking) was removed during the scoring process.

A Lexile Score of **350 to 550** is appropriate for the third-grade independent reading level.

A Lexile Score of **500 to 700** is appropriate for the fourth-grade independent reading level.

Preparing for Difficult or Unfamiliar Text

To assess fluency, have students read text that is new to them (Blevins, 2001). With this in mind, when using the plays for assessment, do not prepare students by introducing unfamiliar or difficult words. Prereading may distort the assessment results.

Before reading for the purpose of *developing* fluency, however, it is helpful to highlight words that may prove to be stumbling blocks for struggling readers. Words slightly above grade level, difficult words on grade level, and complex high-frequency words can be daunting when encountered for the first time within text. To prevent this, introduce words and help students decode them before they read. Give them a chance to decipher the words before you provide correct pronunciation. Then review the words several times to aid recognition and boost fluency.

Using Readers Theater

Readers Theater offers a fun, interactive way to build fluency. Performing can be exciting, and the drive to present well can be a powerful force behind mastering fluency in reading and speech, motivating both struggling and proficient readers. By reading, rehearsing, and performing scripts at their independent reading levels, readers learn to navigate and use the written word in exciting, amusing, and purposeful ways. Readers Theater motivates students to experiment with language, working with expression, pacing, tone, inflection, meaning, and interpretation. To enhance the experience of Readers Theater consider these tips:

Limit Props

Props can distract readers and hinder the success of fluent reading. If you do include them, make them simple and easy to hold. Since scripts are meant to be read aloud rather than memorized, it is important that every reader has one hand free to hold the script.

Treat Scripts as Stories

With the purpose of building strong readers ever in sight, treat the text of a play in much the same way as the text of a story. Read the title with students. Anticipate what the play might be about, and predict outcomes, conflicts, and character behaviors. Invite students to tell how they feel about the plot of the play. See A Fluency Mini-Lesson, page 11, for more ideas on using the plays to boost reading skills.

Heed Clues for Direction

Help students recognize hints in both stage directions and dialogue text that indicate physical movement as well as the pitch, emotion, or volume of speech. For example, words spelled in all capital letters are generally intended to be shouted. Stage directions often indicate not only activity (*waving his arms*) but appropriate tone of voice (for example, *sadly*). It's helpful to give audience members copies of the plays so that they can read along.

Develop Prosody

Prosody, or the rhythm of language, comes alive in Readers Theater—but only when readers are able to read their text easily. Students need to read and reread their scripts many times in order to feel comfortable reading their own character's lines and understanding the purpose and flow of the play. Encourage readers to work first in pairs, and then in small groups and individually, to practice the text until they feel comfortable reading it aloud.

Consider Placement

When performing Readers Theater, it's effective for students to stand so they can be seen and heard. Have readers face the person(s) to whom they are speaking, and have the narrator speak directly to the audience. It works well to have all performers "onstage" at once, standing in a semi-circle and facing the audience. As your students grow with Readers Theater, movement and staging can be added to the performance, if desired.

Encourage Teamwork

Encourage readers to pay attention not only to their own lines but to those of fellow performers. Reading along while others speak their lines will promote fluent reading and will ensure that each performer is ready when his or her turn comes along.

Resources for Reading Fluency, Comprehension, and Readers Theater

Armbruster, Bonnie B., Fran Lehr, and Jean Osborn. *Put Reading First: The Research Building Blocks for Teaching Children to Read.* (Center for the Improvement of Early Reading Achievement and the National Institute for Literacy. Office of Educational Research and Improvement, U.S. Department of Education, 2001).

Blevins, Wiley. *Building Fluency: Lessons and Strategies for Reading Success.* New York: Scholastic, 2001.*

Charlton, Beth Critchley. *Informal Assessment Strategies.* Ontario, Canada: Pembroke Publishers, 2005.

Clay, Marie M. *Becoming Literate: The Construction of Inner Control.* Portsmouth, NH: Heinemann, 1991.

Cunningham, Patricia M. and Richard L. Allington. *Classrooms That Work: They Can ALL Read and Write.* New York: Pearson Education, 2003.

Fiderer, Adele. *35 Rubrics & Checklists to Assess Reading and Writing.* New York: Scholastic, 1998.

Fountas, Irene C. and Gay Su Pinnell. *Guiding Readers and Writers.* Portsmouth, NH: Heinemann, 2001.

Heilman, Arthur W. *Phonics in Perspective.* Upper Saddle River, NJ: Pearson Education, 2002.

Lyon, G. Reid. "Why Reading Is Not a Natural Process." *Educational Leadership*, Volume 55, No. 6 (March 1998): pp. 14–18.

Lyon, G. Reid and Vinita Chhabra. "The Science of Reading Research." *Educational Leadership*, Volume 61, No. 6 (March 2004): pp. 12–17.

Pinnell, Gay Su and Patricia L. Scharer. *Teaching for Comprehension in Reading.* New York: Scholastic, 2003.*

Rasinski, Timothy V. "Creating Fluent Readers," *Educational Leadership*, Volume 61, No. 6 (March 2004): pp. 46–51.

Rasinski, Timothy V. *The Fluent Reader.* New York: Scholastic, 2003.

Rasinski, Timothy V. *3-Minute Reading Assessments: Word Recognition, Fluency, and Comprehension, Grades 1–4.* New York: Scholastic, 2005.

Torgesen, J. K. "The Prevention of Reading Difficulties." *Journal of School Psychology*, Volume 40, Issue 1, pp. 7–26.

Worthy, Jo and Karen Broaddus. "Fluency Beyond the Primary Grades: From Group Performance to Silent, Independent Reading." *The Reading Teacher*, Volume 55, No. 4, pp. 334–343.

Worthy, Jo and Kathryn Prater. "I Thought About It All Night: Readers Theatre for Reading Fluency and Motivation (The Intermediate Grades)." *The Reading Teacher*, Volume 56, No. 3 (November 2002): p. 294.

Worthy, Jo. *Readers Theater for Building Fluency.* New York: Scholastic, 2005.

Yopp, Hallie Kay and Ruth Helen Yopp. "Supporting Phonemic Awareness Development in the Classroom." *The Reading Teacher*, Volume 54, No. 2 (October 2000): pp. 130–143.

---

* This resource includes samples and/or examples of phrase-cued text.

Coyote and the Rock

�֍ Adapted from a White River Sioux legend ✦

CHARACTERS

Narrator   Trees
Fox   Bear 1
Coyote   Bear 2
Rock   Wind

Narrator:	One day, Coyote and Fox walked down a long, dusty road.
Fox:	(*stopping to rub one foot*) My feet are getting tired. Let's stop and rest somewhere.
Coyote:	(*pointing to a rock at the side of the road*) That rock is big enough for two of us. Help me spread my blanket over it.

(Coyote and Fox spread the blanket on the rock and lie on it.)

Fox:	There's nothing better than stretching out on a sunny day.
Coyote:	(*stretching*) You said it, Fox. I could relax here all day long.
Narrator:	Hours later, Fox and Coyote awoke.
Fox:	It's hot out here! Let's go find some water to drink.

Fluency Practice Read-Aloud Plays: Grades 3–4 • Scholastic Teaching Resources

Coyote: It's too hot to drag this blanket with us. I'll just leave it here.

Fox: Thank you, Rock. We had a nice nap on your flat surface!

Coyote: (*He drapes the blanket over the rock.*) Keep this blanket as our gift to you.

Narrator: Fox and Coyote walked on down the road. Before long, storm clouds covered the sun. Then rain began to fall.

(*Coyote and Fox begin to run. They hunch over to protect themselves from the rain.*)

Coyote: I'm cold and wet! Let's go get my blanket, Fox.

Narrator: Coyote and Fox ran back to the rock.

Fox: Thanks for watching our blanket, Rock. We need it back now.

Rock: You gave me this blanket as a gift. It's keeping me warm and dry. You can't have it back.

Coyote: You're a ROCK. You don't need a blanket. I'm taking it.

Narrator: Coyote snatched the blanket and wrapped it around himself and Fox. Then he and Fox walked away, down a steep hill.

Fox: (*stopping to listen*) I hear a noise.

Coyote: Wow! Listen to that loud thunder! I've never heard such a—

Fox: (*looking behind, his mouth drops open in surprise*) That's not thunder! It's Rock! He's rolling right at us!

Coyote: (*waving Fox on with his arms*) Quick! Run into the woods!

Trees: We'll protect you!

Narrator: Rock tumbled faster and faster, knocking down trees with a great roar.

Rock: CRASH! I'll flatten anything that gets in my way!

Fox: (*pointing to a pair of bears in the woods*) Look! There are bears over there! They'll protect us!

Bear 1: (*shaking his head and turning to run*) You're on your own, Coyote! That rock is big and mean!

Bear 2: (*running away*) He'll flatten us like pancakes! We're getting out of here!

Rock: (*He stops rolling.*) Give me that blanket, or I'll run you down, too!

Narrator: Fox and Coyote ran through the woods to the edge of a cliff. The rock rolled close behind.

Coyote: (*pointing to a tree hanging over the edge of the cliff*) Hurry, Fox! Grab on to a tree branch!

Narrator: Coyote and Fox leaped up and held on to a tree branch that hung over the edge of the cliff. Rock rolled after them. He rolled so fast that he missed the tree and dropped off the edge of the cliff.

Rock: HELP! I am falling!

Fox: (*looking down*) What a crash landing! Rock broke into a million pieces!

Coyote: It serves him right, being so greedy. (*Coyote and Fox climb down from the tree and stand on the ground.*) Hand me the blanket.

Fluency Practice Read-Aloud Plays: Grades 3–4 Scholastic Teaching Resources

(Coyote wraps the blanket around himself.)

Narrator: Just then, a cold wind blew. It tore the blanket from Coyote's shoulders.

(Coyote tries to grasp the blanket, but the wind carries it away.)

Wind: You are greedy, too, Coyote. You gave a gift and took it back. Now I'm in charge of the blanket. I know some birds who will use it to keep their babies warm.

Coyote: *(jumps up to try and grab the blanket back)* You can't have that! It's mine! You're worse than Rock!

Narrator: Wind carried the blanket over the cliff and up, up into the sky. Soon the blanket disappeared from sight.

Fox: *(shrugging his shoulders)* Not much to do at the edge of this cliff. What do you say we turn back and take a walk, Coyote?

 THE END

The Missing Trophy

CHARACTERS

Narrator	Stacy
Mrs. Vito	Nora
Ian	Mr. Nash
Willis	Paula
Kira	Armen

Narrator: One Monday morning, the principal of Summit School made a troubling announcement.

(*Students are sitting in their classroom, listening.*)

Mrs. Vito: (*over the loudspeaker*) Last week, our soccer team won the state championship and received a fabulous trophy. Today that trophy is missing!

Ian: (*turning to Nora*) A mystery to solve!

Willis: (*loudly, to the class*) We won that trophy because of me! I should have kept it at my house!

Kira: That trophy was nothing but a reason to show off!

Willis: Kira, you're just jealous because you didn't make the soccer team, and we won the championship.

Stacy: (*giving a disgusted look*) That wasn't nice, Willis.

Willis: (*feeling bad about what he said*) I'm sorry, Kira.

Fluency Practice Read-Aloud Plays: Grades 3–4 • Scholastic Teaching Resources

Narrator:	At lunchtime, Ian and Nora talk with Mrs. Vito.
Ian:	(*to Mrs. Vito*) Nora and I are good at solving mysteries. We want to find the missing trophy. When did it disappear?
Mrs. Vito:	The trophy was in the display case on Friday. It was still there on Saturday when I locked the doors after the basketball games. This morning, I unlocked the doors. I noticed right away that the trophy was gone.
Nora:	(*taking notes*) Was the case open? Was it broken?
Mrs. Vito:	No. The case was closed and locked.
Ian:	We're going to help you close this case, Mrs. Vito.
Narrator:	Outside the office, Nora and Ian go over the clues.
Ian:	Mrs. Vito saw the trophy when she locked the school doors on Saturday. It was gone when she came in on Monday. That means the crime happened Sunday.
Nora:	And the case wasn't broken and was even locked. Whoever took the trophy had a key.

(*Ian and Nora study the school calendar. Ian points to Sunday.*)

Ian:	Sunday was the day Mr. Nash set up the book fair! He would have needed a key to get into the school!
Narrator:	Ian and Nora find Mr. Nash at the copy machine.
Ian:	Hi, Mr. Nash. You set up the book fair on Sunday, right?
Mr. Nash:	Yes, that's right.
Ian:	Did you work alone?

Mr. Nash: No. Armen helped me for an hour and then played basketball in the gym. Kira and Stacy helped, too.

Nora: Thanks, Mr. Nash.

(Ian and Nora walk away. They find Kira in the classroom.)

Nora: Hi, Kira. We're helping find out who took the trophy.

Kira: Why don't you ask Willis? He always said he wanted his own trophy. I'll bet he took it.

Nora: What did you do when you got here yesterday?

Kira: I went to the book fair with Stacy. We unpacked boxes for a while. I was in charge of the craft books.

Ian: Craft books?

Narrator: Kira held up a book fair flyer and pointed to a picture.

Kira: Books that teach you how to make crafts. See this pipe cleaner animal kit? I put out a ton of those.

(Kira opens the door and steps outside. Willis and Stacy run in.)

Willis: Hey, Ian. Hey, Nora. What's up?

Ian: We're trying to find the trophy.

Willis: That trophy should have belonged to me. I worked harder than anyone else. I scored three goals to win!

Nora: Where were you on Sunday?

Willis: The team had practice and a pizza party. Why?

Fluency Practice Read-Aloud Plays: Grades 3–4   Scholastic Teaching Resources

Ian:	Just wondering. Stacy, were you at school yesterday?
Stacy:	(*nodding*) Yes. I help set up the book fair every year.
Nora:	How did you help?
Stacy:	First I worked at the craft table with Kira. Then Armen helped me set up picture books.
Narrator:	Just then, the school bell rang.
Ian:	It's time to go to the book fair. Everyone's lining up!
Narrator:	Nora stands in line at the fair. In front of her, a girl holds a book fair flyer and talks to Mr. Nash.
Paula:	I'm looking for the pipe cleaner animal kits. They show them in the flyer, but I can't find them.
Mr. Nash:	Those didn't come in yet, Paula. There was a mistake, and they won't be here until tomorrow. (*looking around*) Where did I put my keys this time?
Nora:	(*She pays for two books and then walks over to Armen.*) Armen, I have a question.
Armen:	If it's about that trophy, I didn't take it. I helped set up, played basketball, and then set up again. That's it. You know I'm not into sports, Nora. Why would I steal a trophy?
Nora:	(*She whispers to Ian.*) Come on. We have to see Mrs. Vito again. I know who took the trophy.
Narrator:	In Mrs. Vito's office, Kira glares at Ian and Nora.

Kira: I was upset that I didn't make the team! When I saw that trophy every day, I got angry. Then Mr. Nash left his keys on the table at the book fair, so I used them. I put the keys back after I hid the trophy.

Mrs. Vito: Thanks for your help, Ian and Nora. You may go back to class.

Ian: (*walking down the hall with Nora*) Well, another case solved.

Nora: We'd better find Mr. Nash and tell him to hang onto his keys! He'll never believe where they've been!

 THE END

The Wolf and the Seven Young Kids

Fluency Practice Read-Aloud Plays: Grades 3–4   Scholastic Teaching Resources

CHARACTERS

Narrator 1	Willy Wolf
Narrator 2	Greg
Mother Goat	Gus
Gail	Guy
Greta	Gabby
Gary	

Narrator 1:   There once lived a kind mother goat who had seven kids. She loved them dearly.

Narrator 2:   One day, the mother called to her children.

Mother Goat: Children, come close. I have something to tell you.

(*The seven kids gather around their mother by the door.*)

Mother Goat: I need to go into town and run some errands this morning. You will be here alone while I am gone.

Gail: Don't worry, Mom. We'll be fine.

Mother Goat: I do worry, Gail, for hungry wolves live in these woods and one might try to come after you.

Greta: We'll stay inside and won't let anyone in.

Mother Goat: There's one wolf I know who is very clever. He may try to trick you into letting him in. I warn you: DO NOT OPEN THE DOOR UNLESS YOU HEAR MY SOFT, SWEET VOICE AND SEE MY WHITE PAWS THROUGH THE WINDOW.

Gary: We'll be careful. That wolf won't fool us.

Narrator 1:   The mother goat waved good-bye and set off to town.

Narrator 2:   Just down the road, the wolf saw the mother go by and knew that her children must be home alone.

Willy Wolf: (*licking his lips*) Ah, I sense a tasty meal. Those kids know nothing of me. This will be a snap.

(*The wolf walks up to the door of the cottage and knocks. Startled, the seven kids gather by the door.*)

Greg: (*loudly*) Who is it?

Willy Wolf: (*in a loud, deep voice*) It's your mother. I forgot something. Go ahead and let me in.

Greta: (*whispering to the others*) That voice isn't soft or sweet! That's not our mother. It's the wolf!

Gail: Our mother's voice is soft and sweet! Yours is rough and loud, like the voice of a wolf! Go away!

Willy Wolf: (*to himself as he walks away*) Darn! I should have thought of that! I'd better do something about it.

Narrator 1:   The wolf went to town and bought some thick sticks of chalk. He ate these to coat his throat and make his voice softer and sweeter.

Fluency Practice Read-Aloud Plays: Grades 3–4 • Scholastic Teaching Resources

Narrator 2:	Then the wolf went back to the cottage and knocked on the door.

(The seven kids gather by the door again.)

Gus:	(*loudly*) Who is it?
Willy Wolf:	(*He places his paw on the windowpane beside the door to steady himself. Then he takes a deep breath and speaks in a soft, high-pitched voice.*) It's me, and I'm back from the store. I saw a wolf running into town and came back to check on you! Are you all right?
Gus:	(*about to turn the doorknob and open the door*) Mom!
Guy:	(*pointing toward the window*) WAIT! That paw on the window! It's brown! Mom's paws are white.
Gail:	That paw belongs to the wolf!
Gus:	Go away, Wolf! We know it is you! Your paws are dirty and brown. Our mother's are clean and white.
Willy Wolf:	(*walking away from the door*) Foiled again! AHHH! I should have thought of that!
Narrator 1:	The wolf raced into town. He knew the mother goat would soon be home, and he needed to hurry.
Narrator 2:	The wolf stepped into a bakery.
Willy Wolf:	(*sharply*) Quick! I need a bowl of flour right away! Get it now or I'll eat you!
Narrator 1:	The baker gave the wolf a bowl of flour on the spot.
Willy Wolf:	(*rolling his paws in the flour*) Nice and white, just like their mother's. Now, I must get back there!

Fluency Practice Read-Aloud Plays: Grades 3–4   Scholastic Teaching Resources

Narrator 2:   The wolf ran back to the cottage, placed one white paw on the window, and knocked on the door.

(*Once again, the kids huddle by the door.*)

Gabby: Who is it?

Willy Wolf: (*He speaks in a sweet, soft voice but is breathing quickly, as if out of breath.*) My goodness! The baker said he saw a wolf running toward our cottage. Quick! Let me in and I'll protect you!

Gabby: (*to the others*) It's Mom! Hear her sweet, soft voice!

Gus: (*pointing to the window*) And see her clean, white paw!

Greta: (*opening the door*) Mom! Thank goodness you're—

(*The seven kids scream and run around the cottage as the wolf leaps through the doorway. Growling, the wolf chases the kids and eats six of them.*)

Narrator 1:   The wolf chased the kids around the cottage and caught all but one. The youngest kid, Gabby, hid behind a chair, and the wolf did not see her.

Willy Wolf: (*walking out of the cottage*) Now that's what I call a great meal! I'm so full! I need to lie down! (*The wolf lies under a tree and begins to snore.*)

Narrator 2:   Before long, the mother goat came home. She saw the open door, threw down her bags, and raced inside.

Mother Goat: (*frantically calling out*) Gail? Greta? Gary? My children, where are you? Greg! Gus! Guy! Where can you be? My little Gabby?

Gabby: (*Afraid, she peeks out from behind the chair. Then she jumps up and races into her mother's arms.*) I am here! (*crying*) The nasty wolf ate everyone else! They are gone!

Mother Goat: What was I thinking? I should have taken you all into town with me! How could I have left you alone? My babies!

Gabby: (*looks out the front door and points*) There he is! There is the wolf that ate my brothers and sisters!

(*Mother Goat walks close to the wolf and stares at him angrily.*)

Narrator 1: The mother goat noticed that the wolf's stomach was large and bulging. Then she saw something strange.

Mother Goat: Gabby, look! His stomach is moving! Could my babies be in there... and be alive?

Narrator 2: In a flash, the mother goat whipped out her best carving knife and opened the stomach of the sleeping wolf. Out jumped her six kids, all happy to see their mother.

Mother Goat: Quick, children! Bring some large rocks.

(*The children bring the rocks to their mother. She puts them in the wolf's stomach and sews it closed again.*)

Mother Goat: (*sewing the last stitch*) That ought to do it! Now when that wolf wakes up, he'll have a tummy full of rocks, not kids! Come on! Let's go to the meadow. We'll have a picnic!

Narrator 1: And so the family skipped happily off to the meadow.

Narrator 2: And the wolf? Well, let's just say he was a little weighed down. He dragged himself into the woods and was never seen or heard from again.

 THE END

Meeting Thomas Edison

Fluency Practice Read-Aloud Plays: Grades 3–4 Scholastic Teaching Resources

CHARACTERS

Mr. Lopez

Annie

Will

Trevor

Pam

Narrator

Thomas Edison

Mr. Lopez: Good morning, fourth grade! It's time for another Famous Inventor report! (*He checks his planning book to see whose turn it is.*) It looks like it's time for Thomas Edison's group. (*He looks at Annie and her group.*) Are you ready?

Annie: Yes, our group is ready. That's Trevor, Will, Pam, and me.

(*Will and Annie drag a large cardboard box to the front of the room. The box is decorated with hand-drawn lights, buttons, and clocks, to look like a time-travel machine.*)

Will: (*to the class*) We made this cardboard box look like a time machine.

Trevor: (*to the class*) Please turn on your imaginations.

Pam: (*to the class*) And join us as we take you back in time!

Narrator:	Trevor, Annie, Will, and Pam climb into the box. Will presses a plastic button. Lights flash, and the box spins around.
Trevor:	What's happening? What's going on?
Will:	I don't know! This thing isn't real! It's not supposed to work!
Narrator:	The box stops shaking, and the group climbs out.
Annie:	(*gasping*) This isn't our classroom! Where are we?
Pam:	I hear footsteps! Someone's coming!
Thomas Edison:	(*excited*) What a day! What a day! (*He bumps into Will.*)
Will:	Oh, excuse me! Who are you?
Thomas Edison:	I'm Thomas Edison. Pleased to meet you. It's dark in this hallway. Come into my study where we can talk.
Narrator:	The children follow Thomas Edison into a little room. A small yellow light glows on a table top.
Annie:	(*pointing at something*) What a funny-looking lamp!
Thomas Edison:	That's not a lamp. It's my new light bulb!
Trevor:	Are you *the* Thomas Edison, inventor of the light bulb?
Thomas Edison:	I didn't invent the light bulb; I just made it better. The first light bulbs got too hot and burned out quickly. I found a way to make bulbs that don't use as much electricity. They don't get too hot, so they last longer.
Will:	If you are Thomas Edison, then our time machine must really work. We've gone back in time! What year is this?

Thomas Edison:	It's 1913. But travel through time isn't possible!
Annie:	We're as surprised as you are!
Pam:	Nice work on your light. It's a big hit in the future.
Trevor:	In the future, you're in the Inventor's Hall of Fame!
Thomas Edison:	I am? Well, how about that! Why don't you stay for a while? I'll show you the phonograph and some of my other inventions.

(He leads the children around the room, pointing out various inventions.)

Will:	*(pointing)* Hey! There's the telegraph that you made!
Thomas Edison:	I didn't invent the telegraph; I made it better. I invented a telegraph that allowed two messages to be transmitted at the same time. Before that, only one could be sent at a time.
Pam:	*(walking over to another invention)* And here's the phonograph! You invented that, too, Mr. Edison?
Thomas Edison:	I did. Then I used the phonograph along with another one of my inventions, a moving-picture machine. Can you guess what I did by using the phonograph and moving-picture machine together?
Trevor:	You made the first talking moving pictures . . . what we call movies! We're doing a report on your inventions, and that's what I liked the best.
Thomas Edison:	*(chuckling)* I can't even imagine what inventions you kids use in your time!

Will:	Our movies, music CD's, and light bulbs…we can trace them all back to your work, Mr. Edison! The future is a lot more entertaining—and bright—thanks to you!
Pam:	But right now, we'd better get back to the future. We're in the middle of a group report!
Annie:	It's been a privilege to meet you, Mr. Edison. I wish we could stay and see more!
Thomas Edison:	I've enjoyed meeting you, too. Good luck with your report. And remember: even when my inventions didn't work, I kept on trying. That's the key to success!
Narrator:	The kids jump into the box and push the button.
Trevor:	Goodbye, Mr. Edison! Thank you for your time!
Narrator:	Just as before, lights flash and the box spins around. When it finally stops, Trevor, Annie, Will, and Pam step out.
Will:	We're back in our classroom! Why is everyone clapping?
Mr. Lopez:	Well done! Well done! You did a great job on your play! Now we know more about Thomas Edison's work. In fact, we could almost feel him in the room!
Trevor:	(*to Annie, Will, and Pam*) Was that for real?
Pam:	I don't know what just happened, but Mr. Lopez sure looks happy. Maybe we'll get an A on this!
Will:	(*clapping*) Let's hear it for time travel!

 **THE END**

Midnight at Old Truman's

CHARACTERS

Narrator

The Turkeys:

   Tremendous Tom

   Willy

   Annabel

   Herman

   Rose

The People:

   Old Truman

   Millie Truman

Narrator:	It is midnight at Old Truman's Turkey Farm. Inside the farm house, Old Truman and his wife, Millie, are fast asleep. Outside, no one is sleeping. The turkeys have all gathered into one barn for a meeting.
Tremendous Tom:	It's November, and you know what that means.
Willy:	(*groaning*) Thanksgiving comes in November, and people want turkeys on their tables.
Tremendous Tom:	Turkeys to EAT at their Thanksgiving feasts. Are we going to let that happen to us?
All Turkeys:	(*shouting*) No!
Tremendous Tom:	Are we going to let Old Truman and his wife make us someone's dinner?
All Turkeys:	(*shouting*) No!

Fluency Practice Read-Aloud Plays: Grades 3–4 · Scholastic Teaching Resources

Tremendous Tom:	That's right. Tonight, we must escape!
Annabel:	(*raising a wing*) Excuse me, Tom. Did you say tonight?
Tremendous Tom:	Right now.

(*The turkeys gobble with excitement.*)

Tremendous Tom:	In five minutes, we're going to gobble loudly. Make as much noise as you can! We need to make Old Truman come running. When he opens the barn door, we'll run past him. He won't be able to stop us.
Herman:	What about the wire fence outside?
Tremendous Tom:	Old Truman won't remember to close that behind him. It's late! He's sleepy. Ready? Set? Start gobbling!

(*The turkeys begin to gobble loudly.*)

Old Truman:	(*sitting up in bed*) Millie! Do you hear that? The turkeys are going wild! There must be a fox near the barn!
Narrator:	Old Truman pulled on his boots and ran outside. He opened the door to the barn where he had heard the noise.
Old Truman:	What's going on in here?
Narrator:	The turkeys run past Old Truman and out to the gate.
Willy:	Old Truman shut the gate! We can't get out!
Old Truman:	(*shaking his head*) Trying to run away? Poor turkeys. I'm sorry, but I just can't set you free. Thanksgiving's right around the corner, and this is a turkey farm.

Narrator:	Old Truman leads the turkeys back to their barn. Then he shuts the gate behind him and goes back to bed.
Narrator:	The next night, the turkeys gather again.
Tremendous Tom:	Okay, Turkeys! We're going to try again!
Rose:	I almost got crushed last night! My wings still hurt!
Tremendous Tom:	Would you rather have an aching wing or a special place on someone's kitchen table?
Rose:	Definitely the wing. Sorry, Tom.
Tremendous Tom:	Okay! This time, we'll make noise again. When Old Truman comes out, we'll run to the giant hole Willy and I chewed in the fence this afternoon!
Annabel:	An escape hole! That's exciting!
Tremendous Tom:	It's right behind the turkey barn. Remember. Make as much noise as you can. Then run for it!

(*The turkeys gobble louder than before.*)

Narrator:	Again, Old Truman runs out to the barn. When the turkeys run past him, Old Truman follows.
Willy:	The hole is patched! We can't get through it!
Old Truman:	What are you turkeys up to? I patched that hole today. I thought the goats chewed on it for lunch. Now I wonder . . .
Narrator:	Once again, Old Truman herded the birds to the barn. With all doors and gates shut, he went back to bed.

Fluency Practice Read-Aloud Plays: Grades 3–4 Scholastic Teaching Resources

Old Truman:	(*to his wife*) Call me crazy, Millie, but I think those turkeys know it's almost Thanksgiving. I think they're trying to run away!
Millie Truman:	(*sleepily*) Oh, Honey, don't be silly. Turkeys can't know about things like that. And they can't make plans to run away, either. It's just not what turkeys do.
Narrator:	The next morning, Millie watched the turkeys closely.
Millie Truman:	(*to herself*) Those turkeys do look a bit nervous. Truman's right. Maybe they do know Thanksgiving is coming!
Narrator:	Millie Truman had the biggest heart east of Indiana. When she thought about those turkeys fearing for their lives, her heart just melted. She ran and found Old Truman.
Millie Truman:	(*to Old Truman*) Honey, those turkeys are walking in circles out there, not eating a thing. I think they do know. I think they're scared!
Old Truman:	(*thoughtfully*) I agree with you, Millie. But selling turkeys earns us money! We can't just let them go!

(*Millie whispers in Old Truman's ear. They both smile.*)

Narrator:	That night at midnight, the turkeys hold another meeting. This time, the barn door opens without warning and in step Old Truman and Millie.

(*The turkeys gasp.*)

Old Truman:	Millie and I know it's Thanksgiving, and you have a right to be scared. But this year's going to be different.
Millie Truman:	I've been knitting since January. I can sell my scarves for a good price.

Old Truman:	We had a great corn crop this fall. We made enough money to make it through the winter. I'm also good with my hands. I can make chairs and tables to sell.
Annabel:	(*whispering to Rose*) Where is he going with this?
Old Truman:	From now on, Thanksgiving will be a time for our turkeys to celebrate, not to be scared!
Millie Truman:	On Thanksgiving Day, you'll have the best meal you've ever had! We'll feed you the best grain money can buy!
Rose:	(*to Annabel*) Well, I'll be!
Tremendous Tom:	They just want to fatten us up so they can sell us!

(*The turkeys gobble in protest.*)

Old Truman:	(*He holds up a hand.*) I know what you're thinking. Millie and I have been turkey farmers for a long time. We're done with that now, but you can live here as long as you like. We'll feed you and give you a clean barn.
Millie Truman:	But we're not going to sell you. We'll sell scarves instead. And tables and chairs. We'll make the money we need.
Old Truman:	From this day on, every turkey on this farm will celebrate Thanksgiving, not be scared of it!

(*The turkeys gobble with delight.*)

Old Truman:	Good night, good birds. Rest and remember, this Thanksgiving will surely be a happy one for you.

THE END

Fluency Practice Read-Aloud Plays: Grades 3–4 • Scholastic Teaching Resources

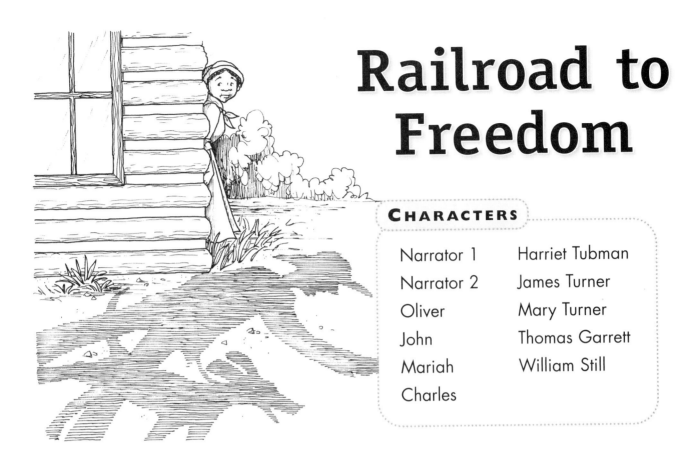

Railroad to Freedom

CHARACTERS

Narrator 1	Harriet Tubman
Narrator 2	James Turner
Oliver	Mary Turner
John	Thomas Garrett
Mariah	William Still
Charles	

Narrator 1: It is a summer night in 1855. Five slaves crouch behind a bush in the woods. They are talking about starting their journey on the Underground Railroad.

Narrator 2: The Underground Railroad is a series of paths that slaves walk on to take them from slavery in southern states to freedom in the north.

Narrator 1: People who know the way lead the slaves and are called conductors. Harriet Tubman is one of the most famous conductors on the Underground Railroad.

Oliver: Tonight is the night! Harriet Tubman is coming for us.

John: She's the only slave I know who really escaped.

Mariah: I can't believe she's coming back to take us north with her!

Oliver: Northern states are free states! We won't be slaves when we get there!

Charles: The journey north will be long and difficult.

Fluency Practice Read-Aloud Plays: Grades 3–4   Scholastic Teaching Resources

| **Mariah:** | Nothing can be as hard as being a slave. I'll risk my life to be free. |
| **Oliver:** | Follow me, then. Watch your step! Even the snap of a twig can give us away. |

(*They walk cautiously through the woods.*)

Harriet Tubman:	(*stepping out from behind a tree*) Welcome, friends. Walk quickly and quietly, and do as I say. One wrong move could mean death for us all.
Narrator 2:	Harriet leads the way through the woods. The travelers step over logs, duck under tree limbs, and walk all night long. In time, they come to a river.
Harriet Tubman:	See that bridge? When we cross it, crawl under the bushes and hide. It's almost daylight, and slave hunters will be looking for us. Stay hidden until night.

(*The slaves crawl under bushes and curl up on the ground.*)

Narrator 1:	The slaves lie awake, afraid. They feel relieved when night comes.
Harriet Tubman:	Now look for a lantern hanging on a post. That tells us where a safe house is.
John:	(*pointing*) There's a lamp. Let's go up to the door.

(*They walk to the house and knock on the door.*)

| **James Turner:** | (*opens the door and smiles*) Welcome, friends. Come inside! Eat a hot meal and stay here until night comes. |
| **Mary Turner:** | Tonight we will take you to the next stop on the Underground Railroad. |

Fluency Practice Read-Aloud Plays: Grades 3–4 • Scholastic Teaching Resources

(The group walks down the stairs to a cellar and lies down on blankets on the floor.)

Charles: How can I sleep? I hear dogs howling. That means the slave hunters are looking for us!

Harriet Tubman: You are safe here. Try to rest, for we still have a long way to travel.

Narrator 2: That night, Harriet and the slaves hide in a wagon filled with hay. James and Mary drive them to the city of Wilmington, Delaware.

(Mariah steps out of the wagon and stares in awe at the town.)

Mariah: I've never seen such a place! So many people and houses!

Narrator 1: A man walks up to the wagon and introduces himself.

Thomas Garrett: My name is Thomas Garrett. I am happy to help you. Come with me.

Harriet Tubman: *(to the slaves)* We are in good hands, my friends. Thomas has been working on the Underground Railroad for more than forty years!

(The slaves and Harriet follow Thomas into the woods. They walk a long way.)

Narrator 2: Thomas leads the group to Philadelphia, Pennsylvania.

Oliver: Pennsylvania is a free state! We are no longer slaves!

Thomas Garrett: You still have a long way to go. *(He gestures to a man who has just approached the group.)* This is my friend William Still. He will lead you on from here. Good-bye, and good luck.

William Still: *(in a serious tone)* Please listen carefully. Even in free states, people hunt runaway slaves. You must go to Canada to be truly free.

Narrator 1:   With William's help, Harriet and the others travel toward Canada.

(The group walks for a long time. They walk with effort, struggling against foul weather.)

Mariah: We've walked hundreds of miles in wind, rain, and snow.

John: We've even hiked over mountains! How much longer must we travel?

Harriet Tubman: Look across Lake Erie! There is Canada, where you can live freely.

Mariah: Lake Erie is huge and filled with chunks of ice! How will we get across?

Harriet Tubman: Jump from one ice floe to the next.

Charles: That's really dangerous! We can't do that!

Harriet Tubman: You have no choice. Slave hunters will find you here. Now get moving!

Narrator 2:   Finally, they reach land in Canada.

Harriet Tubman: Now you are free to find a job, buy land, and build a house! I wish you well!

Narrator 1:   Harriet worked as a conductor on the Underground Railroad from 1851 to 1860. In that time, she traveled to Maryland nineteen times and led about 300 slaves to freedom. People still consider Harriet Tubman one of the bravest women in history.

 THE END

Fluency Practice Read-Aloud Plays: Grades 3–4 • Scholastic Teaching Resources

Go West with the Best!

> ### CHARACTERS
>
> | | | |
> |---|---|---|
> | Narrator | Amanda Deering | Maggie Deering |
> | Lucy Taggard | Carl Deering | Mary Deering |
> | William Brown | | |

Narrator: The year is 1849. Lucy Taggard is standing in the center of a bustling town, shouting to people who pass by.

Lucy Taggard: Fixing to go west to look for gold? Come to Taggard's Trading Post, your Conestoga connection!

William Brown: (*tipping his hat*) Good morning, Lucy. At it again, are you?

Lucy Taggard: A gal has to make money, Mr. Brown.
(*shouting again*) Go west with the best!
My covered wagons are the finest ones around.
Come on over and see.

William Brown: Well, I might just have some business for you. My niece, Amanda, is looking for a wagon. Here she comes now with her family.

Amanda Deering: I'd like to see your wagons, Lucy. My husband and I are fixing to take the girls out west next month, and we'll need a sturdy wagon to make the trip.

Lucy Taggard: How about this fine, covered wagon? It carries up to 2,000 pounds!

Amanda Deering: (*giggling*) I feed my family well, but they don't weigh that much!

Lucy Taggard: (*chuckling*) Amanda, this wagon will hold you, your family, and everything you want to take west. You can even bring your rocking chair!

Amanda Deering: It sure looks strong.

Lucy Taggard: All my wagons are strong. I make them out of hickory, oak, or maple wood! You can take your pick!

Amanda Deering: What's this piece of wood sticking out from the front?

Lucy Taggard: That's called a tongue. It's where you hook up your cattle. You can pull my wagons with mules, horses, or oxen. There's room for up to four animals!

Amanda Deering: We have four oxen at home. My husband, Carl, says oxen are stronger than horses or mules. Here comes Carl now.

Carl Deering: Nice wagon, Lucy. What do you have for covers?

Lucy Taggard:	I sell only the best canvas, Carl.
Maggie Deering:	What do we need canvas for, Daddy?
Carl Deering:	(*pointing*) See those hoops on Lucy's wagons?
Maggie Deering:	One…two…three…four…I see seven hoops!
Carl Deering:	When you stretch canvas over those seven hoops, it makes a roof. The canvas keeps out the hot sun, just like the roof on our old home.
Lucy Taggard:	It keeps out water, too, Honey. Your daddy can rub that whole canvas with oil before he puts it on. Raindrops roll off a well-oiled canvas. Not one lick of water soaks through. The wagon stays dry, and so do you!
Mary Deering:	See all those hooks hanging down from the hoops? What are they for?
Lucy Taggard:	They're for hanging things, Sweetness. You can use those hooks to hang pots, pans, tools, buckets, clothes, and anything else you want to put up there.
Mary Deering:	Like my mama's mixing pots?
Lucy Taggard:	Like your mama's mixing pots. (*She smiles at Amanda and Carl.*) So, are you folks ready to buy?
William Brown:	(*studying the wheels*) I have a question, Lucy. These wheels are made of wood. What if they get dried out or muddy and have trouble turning? I wouldn't want Amanda and Carl to get stuck on the trail!

Lucy Taggard:	(*She holds up a metal bucket.*) Just hang this big bucket of grease on the back of the wagon, Carl. When those wagon wheels start turning slow, you just grease them good. You'll zip down the trail after that!
Amanda Deering:	Well, you've covered almost everything! Except... how much do your wagons cost, Lucy?
Lucy Taggard:	The one you're looking at will run you about 200 dollars.
Amanda Deering:	That sounds like a lot.
Lucy Taggard:	I guarantee that my wagons are worth the price, Amanda. Any one of mine will take you out west... and back if you start feeling homesick!
Carl Deering:	Your wagons are the finest around, Lucy. We'll take one. When can you have it ready for us?
Lucy Taggard:	Place your order today, and I'll deliver your wagon next week.
Carl Deering:	It's a deal.
Lucy Taggard:	(*shaking hands with Carl and Amanda*) Thank you, Amanda and Carl. (*She hands candy to Maggie and Mary.*) And here's some candy for you girls. I'm mighty pleased to have your business, and I'm sure my wagon will serve you well! I wish you the best!

 THE END

Fluency Practice Read-Aloud Plays: Grades 3–4 Scholastic Teaching Resources

The Bremen Town Musicians

CHARACTERS

Narrator	Dog	Robber 2
Cat	Rooster	Robber 3
Donkey	Robber 1	Robber 4

Narrator: On a long, dusty road, a donkey walks slowly toward Bremen Town.

(*The donkey stops walking and sighs. A cat sits nearby, and she notices him.*)

Cat: Why so sad, Donkey?

Donkey: (*sadly*) For 20 years, I plowed the earth for my master, hauled heavy logs, and never once complained! While he ate rich steaks and soups, I gnawed on grass and bitter weeds. After all these years, my back aches terribly, I am weak from lack of food, and what does my master say? He says I am good for nothing now, and he plans to get rid of me!

Cat: So you're leaving?

Donkey: That's right. I'm traveling to Bremen Town. There it won't matter that I'm old or weak or tired, for I'm going to be a musician. I'll make music for everyone to hear!

Fluency Practice Read-Aloud Plays: Grades 3–4   Scholastic Teaching Resources

Cat: (*sadly*) I wish I could be a musician. (*sighing*) My mistress used to say I had the most beautiful voice she'd ever heard.

Donkey: Where is your mistress now?

Cat: (*pointing toward a house at the top of a hill*) She lives in that house. I used to live there, too, where I worked hard and caught twelve mice a day. My mistress fed me sweet cream for a treat. Then I grew older and weaker, and now I am too tired to catch mice. My mistress says I am of no use to her.

Donkey: (*excited*) Then come with me to Bremen Town! We can make music together!

Cat: I think I will!

(*She walks down the road beside the donkey.*)

Narrator: Not far down the road, they pass a dog lying in the sun.

Donkey: Hi! Don't you look calm and cozy on this fine summer day!

Dog: I may look cozy, but inside I am upset. My master is getting rid of me. He used to feed me bones and take me hunting. He scratched my ears and kept me by his side night and day. Now he says I am old and I do nothing. He has no use for me.

Cat: Then you must come with us! We're on our way to Bremen Town to make music!

Dog: I've been to Bremen Town, and it's one busy place! I'll bet lots of people would let us make music for them!

Narrator: And so the donkey, the cat, and the dog trot down the road. Before long, they hear a rooster crow.

Rooster: (*standing alone*) Cock-a-doodle Doo! Oh, I feel so blue!

(*The donkey, the cat, and the dog stop to talk with the rooster.*)

Donkey: Did we hear you say you feel blue? Why are you so sad?

Rooster: I used to run this old farm. When I crowed before sunrise, the farmer woke up to feed the chickens, milk the cows, and gather the eggs! Without me, he would not have done so much work in a day!

Cat: Don't you crow anymore?

Rooster: The farmer and his family use alarm clocks now, so they don't need me. Last night, I saw the farmer reading recipe books to see how he might cook me in a stew!

Dog: (*gasping*) That's terrible! You'd better come with us!

Rooster: Where are you going?

Donkey: We're on our way to Bremen Town to make music.

Rooster: Music? I've been singing all my life!

Cat: Well, come with us then! We'll all be musicians!

Narrator: And so the group heads down the road toward Bremen Town. When night falls, they grow cold and hungry.

Donkey: (*pointing to a farmhouse nearby*) There's a farmhouse up ahead, and the lights are on. Maybe we can sleep there for the night.

Narrator: The four walk up to the farmhouse. The rooster is just about to knock on the door when the cat stops him.

Cat: (*whispering*) Wait! Let's look in the windows first!

(*The animals peek in different windows.*)

Narrator: Inside the house, four robbers feast on chicken, steak, fish, squash, and potatoes. A huge bag of gold sits on the table.

Rooster: I see four men at a table. Look at the size of that bag of gold!

Donkey: And look at the food they're eating! The table is loaded!

Dog: Well, if we're going to be musicians for a living, we ought to start right now. Let's sing for our supper!

Narrator: Very loudly, the donkey begins to bray, the cat to meow, the dog to bark, and the rooster to crow. They sing at the top of their lungs. Inside the house, the robbers hear them.

Robber 1: (*He stops eating and looks up.*) What's that racket?

Robber 2: (*looking out the window*) It's dark. I can't see a thing!

Robber 3: (*covering his ears*) Make it stop! That racket is awful!

Robber 4: What kind of creature makes noises like that?

Robber 1: Is it a monster?

Robber 2: Shut off the lights! Maybe it will think we've gone away.

Narrator: Outside the farmhouse, the animals see the lights go out.

Cat: Hey! The lights went out! Maybe they want us to come in.

Dog: Shutting off the lights is a funny way of asking someone in.

Donkey: Let's go in and introduce ourselves. (*He pushes open the door.*)

Narrator: The animals step into the house. They keep singing, which frightens the robbers and causes them to scramble around in the darkness.

Robber 1: I've got one! Wait! He's got my leg!

Fluency Practice Read-Aloud Plays: Grades 3–4   Scholastic Teaching Resources

Dog: (*holding the first robber's pants leg with his teeth*) Grrr! Grrr! Arf! Arf! Your pants leg will be my scarf!

Robber 2: (*wrestling with the donkey*) OUCH! This thing is kicking me!

Donkey: (*wrestling with Robber 2*) Hee haw! Hee haw! Let go of my jaw!

Robber 3: (*waving his arms*) I can't breathe! I can't breathe!

Rooster: (*flapping his wings in the third robber's face*) Cock-a-doodle! Doodle-dee! Quit swinging your arms at me!

Robber 4: (*trying to pull the cat off his shoulders*) Help! This monster has sharp claws!

Cat: Meow! Meow! Let go of me now!

Robber 1: (*grabbing the bag of gold*): Head for the door!

Narrator: The four robbers break free, and run out the door. They run and run until they are far, far away from the farmhouse.

Donkey: (*turning on a light*) Well, they sure left in a hurry.

Cat: (*sitting down at the table*) I guess they didn't like our singing. (*She takes a bite of fish.*) That's too bad.

Dog: (*eyeing a juicy steak*) Do you think they'll be back?

Rooster: I don't think so. They have their gold, so it seems to me this house is ours now.

Cat: Why move on to Bremen Town when we have a home of our own!

Donkey: See? I told you we'd do well as musicians!

 THE END

Heroine on the Titanic

Fluency Practice Read-Aloud Plays: Grades 3–4   Scholastic Teaching Resources

CHARACTERS

Narrator 1	Narrator 2	Man 2
Margaret Brown	Sailor	Quartermaster Hichens
Sound Crew (three or more students)	Passengers 1–5	Wealthy Man
	Man 1	

Narrator 1:	It is almost midnight on April 14, 1912. Margaret Brown relaxes in her room on the ship Titanic.
Margaret Brown:	(*yawning*) I must get some sleep, but this book is so good that I can't put it down!
Sound Crew:	CRASH!
Narrator 2:	Without warning, the mighty ship heaves, throwing Margaret from her bed onto the floor.
Sound Crew:	KNOCK! KNOCK! KNOCK!
Margaret Brown:	It is almost midnight! Who can be at my door?

(Margaret pulls on her bathrobe and opens the cabin door.)

Sailor: *(handing Margaret a life vest)* Mrs. Brown! Put on a life vest! The ship struck an iceberg and is sinking!

Narrator 1: Margaret pulls on six pairs of wool socks, a wool skirt, a fur coat, and other warm clothes. She puts on the life vest and rushes to the edge of the ship, where hundreds of people crowd on the deck.

Passenger 1: *(screaming)* The ship is sinking!

Passenger 2: *(screaming)* Get out of my way! I need to get into a lifeboat! There aren't enough lifeboats for everyone!

Sailor: Women and children first! Only women and children in the lifeboats!

Passengers 3, 4, and 5: We need to get into a lifeboat, too!

Margaret Brown: Get into this one. See that sailor in the lifeboat? He's helping people climb in. Give him your hand.

Narrator 2: Margaret leads several passengers to the edge of the ship, where others are stepping over the railing and into lifeboats that hang off the ship.

Sailor: *(shouting)* Somebody help me! This woman speaks French, but I don't, and she doesn't understand what I'm saying. She won't get in the boat!

Margaret Brown: I speak French. I'll talk with her.

(Margaret stands in front of the woman and speaks to her kindly.)

Narrator 1:   Margaret convinces the woman to board the lifeboat. Just then, two men on the deck pick Margaret up and carry her to lifeboat number six.

Man 1:   Mrs. Brown! You must go, too!

Margaret Brown: (*struggling to get free*) I cannot go yet! Please save others first!

Man 2:   You must go now, or you will go down with the ship.

Narrator 2:   They force Margaret into the lifeboat and then lower the lifeboat into the water.

Margaret Brown: Wait! This boat is only half-full! Let others get in!

Quartermaster Hichens: It's too late. The Titanic will sink, and the waves will pull us under. We must get away.

Margaret Brown: There is plenty of room in this boat! How can you take care of yourself and leave others to die?

(*The quartermaster looks away without speaking.*)

Margaret Brown: We'll freeze if we just sit here. Give me an oar so I can row! The rest of you must take turns rowing as well. Rowing will keep you from freezing!

(*Margaret and one other passenger begin rowing.*)

Narrator 1:   For two hours, Margaret and the others watch as the ship sinks lower and lower, and its lights go out. In the blackness of night, they hear the wrenching sound of wood splitting apart. Then, silently, the huge ship sinks under the waves and disappears.

Narrator 2:   Twenty lifeboats float on the dark, icy waters of the North Atlantic Ocean.

Passenger 1:   It's freezing out here! I can't take much more.

Margaret Brown: I'm wearing extra socks, sweaters, and furs. I'll take some off, and you can put on what you need.

(*Other passengers put on the extra clothes.*)

Passenger 2:   (*pointing*) I see lights in the distance!

Margaret Brown: Those are lights from a ship! Row to it! Row!

(*Margaret and other passengers row faster and harder.*)

Quartermaster Hichens: We don't need to row anymore. The ship will come to us.

Margaret Brown: Nonsense! We'll freeze to death by the time that ship gets here. Keep rowing!

Narrator 1:   As the sun rises that morning, Margaret's lifeboat reaches the Carpathia, the rescue ship. 2200 people had traveled on the Titanic. Only 706 are rescued.

Narrator 2:   On the ship, Margaret Brown comforts frightened passengers. When the ship reaches New York, Margaret stays on board.

Margaret Brown: (*putting her arm around a frightened young woman*) Your husband will be fine, Honey. Doctors are on their way.

Narrator 1:   She helps families find their loved ones.

Margaret Brown: (*shaking hands with an elderly man and woman*) I was able to reach your daughter by telegram. She's coming to take you home now.

Narrator 2: Margaret also raised money to give to the poorest victims.

Margaret Brown: (*speaking with a wealthy man who hands her a wad of money*) Thank you so kindly, sir. Your donation will help buy food, clothes, and shelter for those who have suffered so much.

Wealthy Man: I'll give more if you need it. How much have you raised, Mrs. Brown?

Margaret Brown: About 10,000 dollars so far.

Wealthy Man: You're doing a wonderful thing to help others.

Margaret Brown: People have lost so much in this tragedy. I'm thankful to be alive.

 **THE END**

Fluency Practice Read-Aloud Plays: Grades 3–4 Scholastic Teaching Resources

Lucky Hans

Based on the fairy tale by the Brothers Grimm

Narrator 1: There once lived a young man named Hans. He was energetic and hardworking, but he lacked common sense.

Narrator 2: For seven years, Hans worked as an apprentice to a miller. He learned to grind wheat and corn into flour. Then one day, the miller came to Hans.

Miller: Hans, you have worked hard for me for seven years and now you are ready to go off on your own. (*He hands Hans a small but heavy nugget of gold.*) Take this gold as payment. It's worth a lot and will feed you and your parents for years.

Narrator 1: Abigail, the miller's daughter, wished Hans well.

Abigail: (*wrapping the gold in a red cloth*) Here, Hans. Let me wrap up this gold so you won't drop it on the way home. It's heavier than it looks!

Hans: (*smiling as he smells Abigail's sweet perfume on the cloth*) Thank you, Abigail. I will never forget you or your kindness to me.

(*The miller and Abigail wave as Hans walks away toward his home.*)

Hans: (*smelling the cloth again and sighing*) Oh, this cloth reminds me so much of Abigail. I'd like to wrap it right around my neck, so it will be near to me.

Narrator 2:   Hans unwrapped the gold and tied the cloth around his neck. Before he could pick up the gold nugget and continue on, a man galloped up on a horse.

Man on a Horse: Good morning, Son! That's a fine chunk of gold you've got there!

Hans: Yes, it looks fine all right. But it's terribly heavy. I've been lugging it home for an hour, and my back's nearly broken.

Man on a Horse: Well, I know it won't be much of a trade for me, but I'd be happy to give you this horse in exchange for your gold. Then you can ride home!

Hans: (*amazed*) Yes! I'd be happy to take your horse for my gold.

(*Hans and the man exchange the horse and gold.*)

Narrator 1:   The man knew he had outwitted Hans, so he grabbed the gold and ran off.

Hans: What a great choice I made, trading that small chunk of gold for this huge horse! My parents will be proud of me.

Narrator 2:   Just then, the horse began to buck. Hans pulled on the reins, and the horse took off.

(*Hans clings to the horse as it races through a field and into someone's backyard.*)

Narrator 1:   The horse carried Hans right into the middle of a wedding! The horse crashed into a table and sent the wedding cake flying into the air.

Bride: Our wedding cake!

Fluency Practice Read-Aloud Plays: Grades 3–4   Scholastic Teaching Resources

Groom: This foolish man has ruined our wedding!

(*The horse gallops away with Hans still on its back.*)

Narrator 2:   The horse ran into a farmyard and threw Hans off his back.

Hans: (*flying through the air*) WHOA!

Narrator 1:   Hans landed right between the horns of a gentle cow, and the horse ran away.

Hans: (*watching the horse run*) Well, I'm glad he's gone! What a dangerous animal! I could have been killed.

Narrator 2:   As Hans climbed off the cow, a farmer arrived.

Farmer: Young man! What are you doing to my cow?

Hans: Nothing, sir. My horse threw me, and I landed on the horns of your cow.

Farmer: (*pointing*) That horse is yours? I'd like to have a horse so fast and strong, and you seem to like my cow. Want to trade?

Narrator 1:   They shook hands, and Hans led the cow away.

Hans: (*to the cow*) I'll take you home with me. My parents will have milk to drink for the rest of their lives.

Narrator 2:   And so, Hans led the cow down the road. He slept beside it in a haystack that night. Several times, Hans tried to milk the cow so he would have something to drink. But the cow would not give milk.

Hans: Well, how do you like that? A cow without milk! What good is a cow that won't give milk?

Narrator 1: Hans saw a pond and decided to swim, but he went out too far and started to sink. Frightened, he threw his arms around a goose.

Hans: Help! Save me! Save me! (*Hans stops and looks closely at the goose.*) Why, you're a plump bird. I'll take you home with me, and tonight my parents and I will feast on roast goose.

Narrator 2: Hans carried the goose down the road until he met a man who carried two heavy grinding stones.

Hans: (*setting down the goose*) Those stones look heavy, sir. Why don't I hold them for you so that you can rest for a while?

Man with the Stones: Why thank you! How very kind.

Narrator 1: The man put the stones down and spied the goose.

Man with the Stones: My goodness, that goose looks plump and tasty. What a fine meal that goose would make!

Hans: I'm taking this goose home to give to my parents. I've been away for seven years.

Man with the Stones: You've been away for seven years, and all you're bringing home is a goose? Your parents are sure to be upset that you've brought them so little. Now, if you brought them these fine grinding stones, then they'd be happy.

Hans: (*thinking*) What you say is true. The goose would be gone in one evening, but the grinding stones would sharpen our farm tools for years! Want to trade?

Fluency Practice Read-Aloud Plays: Grades 3–4 Scholastic Teaching Resources

**Man with
the Stones:** (*pretending to consider the idea*) Well, it wouldn't be much of a trade for me, but okay, I'll do it.

(*The man eagerly picks up the goose and hurries away.*)

Narrator 2: Hans carried the heavy stones to the edge of his family's farm. He placed the stones on a well and leaned in to get a drink.

Narrator 1: As Hans pulled up a bucket of water, his elbow knocked both grinding stones down into the well.

Hans: OH NO! My stones are gone and now I have nothing!

(*Sad at first, Hans walks slowly up the path to his family's cottage. As he grows closer, his cheerful mood returns, and he runs up to the door.*)

Hans: Mother! Father! I'm home at last! After seven years, I've come home!

Father: (*shaking hands and clapping Hans on the back*) Welcome home, Son! What did you earn for your seven years of hard work?

Hans: A nugget of gold, sir!

Father: Splendid! We'll be able to buy food at last. Where is it?

Hans: I don't have it anymore. I traded my gold for a horse and the horse for a cow. Then I left the cow but found a goose, and I traded the goose for two grinding stones which fell into our well. I come to you with nothing. I am sorry.

Mother: (*hugging her son*) Nonsense! You've brought what we missed most of all . . . yourself! Welcome home, Hans.

 THE END

Remembering Uncle Fremont

CHARACTERS

Narrator
Troy Clark
Wendy Bennett
Jay Monroe
Maria Strand
Brad Lewis

Narrator:	One sunny day in November, Wendy Bennett climbed the stairs outside the law office of Troy Clark. She pressed a bell, and a tall man opened the door.
Troy:	(*shaking Wendy's hand*) You must be Ms. Bennett. I'm Troy Clark, your Uncle Fremont's lawyer. Come on in.
Wendy:	(*stepping inside*) Thank you, Mr. Clark. Am I the first one here?
Troy:	Actually, you're the last. Now that you're here, we can begin.
Wendy:	(*walking down the hall with Troy*) I can't believe Uncle Fremont remembered me in his will. Who else is here?
Troy:	(*leading her down a hallway and opening another door*) In here, Ms. Bennett.
Wendy:	(*gasping with surprise and pleasure*) Jay! Brad! Maria! It's been forever!

Fluency Practice Read-Aloud Plays: Grades 3–4 • Scholastic Teaching Resources

Jay: (*hugging Wendy*) For cousins, we don't keep in touch much!

Wendy: (*hugging Brad and Maria*) Uncle Fremont had seventeen nieces and nephews. Why are we the only ones here?

(*The others shake their heads, unsure.*)

Troy: (*holding a letter*) Your uncle wrote this letter, asking me to gather you four for the reading of his will. In an earlier portion of his will, he donated his farmhouse to our town's Historical Society. That house is 200 years old, and the Society's very pleased. (*He picks up a piece of paper and a hair dryer.*) Your uncle insisted that this part of his will be read ONLY with you four present. To be sure it remained private, he wrote the will in invisible ink.

Wendy: Made with lemon juice! I taught Uncle Fremont how to do that!

Troy: The heat from this hair dryer will make the words appear. Here goes.

(*He turns on the dryer and points it at the paper. The others lean forward, watching words appear.*)

Troy: (*reading aloud*) "My dear Wendy, Jay, Brad, and Maria, all your lives, you have shown me great kindness and love. You have brought me more joy than you knew. In love and gratitude, I give you each one-fourth of my fortune. Uncle Fremont." There is a note to me here, asking me to give you these items. Maria, your uncle left you this box of tea bags. Jay, he has left you these work boots, and Brad, your gift is this log.

Maria: What about Wendy?

Troy: That's all I have here. You know your Uncle Fremont; always one for mysteries! (*He winks.*) I believe the Historical Society won't take possession of the house until next week. If you go there today, you might just find your answer! (*He looks at his watch and stands.*) Now if you'll excuse me, I have an appointment in fifteen minutes. It's been a pleasure meeting you.

Narrator: Brad, Jay, Maria, and Wendy leave the building and head straight to Uncle Fremont's farmhouse. They find a key under the front mat and go into his house.

(*Brad, Jay, Maria, and Wendy sit down in the living room.*)

Brad: There's no way these things are the fortune Uncle Fremont left behind. If they had been, he would have left something for you, Wendy. He promised you that in his will.

Jay: (*holding up the work boots*) These must be the clues!

Wendy: He wants us to find the fortune!

Maria: (*holding the box of tea bags*) It's cold in this house. I'll make some tea to warm us up. (*She walks into the kitchen, opens the box, and then rushes back into the living room.*) Hey! This box is full of tea bags from all around the world! Some come from Ireland, England, and Japan—all places I traveled with Uncle Fremont when I was on school vacations! In four years, we had cups of tea in five countries!

Wendy: If tea bags are a clue, then maybe he wants us to look inside the teapot and see what's there!

Maria: (*Back in the kitchen, she lifts the lid on an antique china teapot and calls out.*) There's a key in here!

(*The others hurry into the kitchen.*)

Jay: (*studying the key*) This looks like the key to a desk.

Maria: I recognize that key! It's the key Uncle Fremont always kept in his pocket! But it doesn't fit into a desk. It belongs to that fancy wooden box over the fireplace. I used to hold that box in my lap and wonder what was inside. (*Maria takes the key and opens a small wooden box on the fireplace mantle. She pulls out a stack of letters, neatly tied together.*) I wrote these letters to Uncle Fremont starting when I was eight years old! I can't believe he kept them!

Brad: Your letters must have meant a lot to Uncle Fremont. He lived alone for a long time and must have felt lonely sometimes.

Maria: (*smiling*) He was good to me. (*remembering the clues*) Jay, he left you work boots! What do you think they mean?

Jay: These are the boots Uncle Fremont wore when he taught me to work on his farm. I stayed here for three summers in a row because I loved the farm life so much. Uncle Fremont taught me everything!

(*Jay puts on the work boots and leads the others outside to the barn.*)

Jay: (*pointing*) There's the cornfield I used to help water. And there's the barn where I helped feed the chickens and cows. (*He points to a wide, open field.*) And there . . . there's where I learned to ride a horse and drive a tractor.

(*Brad steps into a woodshed.*)

Brad: Hey, I remember this! This is the woodshed where I helped Uncle Fremont chop wood for the fireplace. Remember those cold winter days that we spent at his house? I used to help Uncle Fremont chop the wood to keep the fireplace going inside and warm up the house. (*He runs his hand over the handle of an axe that is stuck in the wood.*) I thought it was the coolest thing, getting to use this axe!

Narrator: As Brad runs his hand along the axe, he finds an envelope taped to the handle.

Brad: (*opening the envelope*) Hey! Look at this! It's a letter from Uncle Fremont . . . and a key!

Maria: (*excited*) I recognize his handwriting! May I read it?

(*Brad hands the letter to Maria, who clears her throat and reads aloud.*)

Maria: My dear children. I have loved you all my life. You brought joy to a lonely man, and you never stopped caring for me. The fact that you came here and followed my clues shows that our times together meant something to you as well. Because of this, I have left you each one-fourth of my fortune. Go to Madison Bank this afternoon, and use this key to open Safety Deposit Box Number 4970. In there, you will find four envelopes, each with an equal bank check inside. Use this money well, and know that it comes from my heart.

(*All is quiet as the four stand in the woodshed.*)

Brad: (*shaking his head in disbelief*) Time spent with others is never forgotten.

Maria: Not by Uncle Fremont.

Wendy: And not by any of us, either.

Jay: (*quietly*) Let's stay here a while, okay? We can go to the bank later on.

Maria: (*smiling*) Come on inside, and I'll make us that tea.

 **THE END**

Fluency Practice Read-Aloud Plays: Grades 3–4 Scholastic Teaching Resources

About Ten Bowls of Porridge

Fluency Practice Read-Aloud Plays: Grades 3–4   Scholastic Teaching Resources

CHARACTERS

Narrator
Mr. Drake
Brian Drake
Mr. Westcott
Mrs. Drake

Narrator: Once upon a time, in a little English town, a young boy named Brian Drake struggled with math. Try as he might, Brian could never finish his math work in less than two hours.

(*Brian is doing his homework in the kitchen when Mr. Drake comes into the room.*)

Mr. Drake: Brian, you've been doing that schoolwork since four o'clock, and now it's six-forty-five! You've spent almost three hours on one subject!

Brian: Father, I could do this homework for seven hours and still not understand it. My classmates are multiplying and dividing, but I can't even round to the nearest ten!

Mr. Drake: Why, I've always been good at mathematics. I'll help you understand this, but first, where is your mother's porridge pot?

(*Mr. Drake finds the little black pot and puts it on the stove.*)

Brian: You shouldn't use that pot, Father. Last time, the pot made so much porridge that it poured onto the floor, out of our house, and through the whole village! People were digging themselves out for days, and the whole town was angry with us!

Mr. Drake: We didn't know how to talk to the pot back then, but now we do. (*He speaks to the pot.*) Cook, little pot, cook!

Narrator: Instantly, thick, sweet porridge bubbled in the pot.

Mr. Drake: (*handing bowls to Brian*) Please fill these twelve bowls.

Brian: (*filling bowls*) All right, Father, and now can we stop the pot?

Mr. Drake: Nonsense, Son! We're just beginning. You filled twelve bowls, so about how many bowls of porridge are there?

Brian: About ten?

Mr. Drake: Correct! (*He scoops porridge into more bowls.*) Now how many do you see?

Brian: I see sixteen bowls of porridge . . . and a lot more porridge in that pot! It's getting up to the top! Shouldn't we stop?

(*Mr. Drake continues talking as if he did not hear Brian.*)

Mr. Drake: Right again! Sixteen bowls . . . about how many is that?

Brian: Sixteen bowls of porridge is about ten.

Mr. Drake: Think some more, Son, for numbers that end in five or higher must be rounded up.

Brian: So sixteen bowls of porridge would be about twenty?

Mr. Drake: Yes! Now go borrow thirty bowls from our neighbors.

Brian: Thirty bowls!

(*Brian nervously wipes sweat from his forehead and rushes out the front door.*)

Narrator: Five minutes later, Brian comes back with thirty bowls.

Fluency Practice Read-Aloud Plays: Grades 3–4 • Scholastic Teaching Resources

Brian:	(*pointing as he balances the bowls in his arms*) Father, the porridge is boiling over onto the floor!
Narrator:	Mr. Drake sloshes through the porridge, fills the bowls, and lines them up on the table.
Mr. Drake:	Exactly how many bowls of porridge do we have now?
Brian:	(*He talks quickly, trying to hurry his father.*) Sixteen plus thirty is forty-six.
Mr. Drake:	About how many bowls is that?
Brian:	Forty-six is about . . . fifty?
Mr. Drake:	You're getting it, son!
Brian:	We're going to get it when Mother sees this house; there's porridge everywhere! It's a complete mess! I understand rounding now, so can we turn off the pot?
Mr. Drake:	In a minute, after you try a few more. We need more bowls, though.
Brian:	(*shaking his head*) This is unbelievable.
Narrator:	Brian runs out and brings back 83 bowls.
Mr. Drake:	We have 129 bowls, so about how many is that?
Brian:	(*eyeing the door nervously*) That is way too many. It's bubbling down the street, sir.
Mr. Drake:	About how many bowls of porridge is 129?
Brian:	Nine is the last number, so I need to round up to 130.

Narrator:	Porridge continues to stream out of the house and down the street. Mr. Westcott, a neighbor, barges in.
Mr. Westcott:	(*yelling*) Drake, this is outrageous! I can't believe you turned on that foolish pot again! The streets are inundated with that glop, and there's no rain in the forecast to wash it away! Do you know how much the cleanup is going to cost taxpayers in this town? The last time you flooded our streets, it cost sixty-three dollars a family!
Brian:	When you consider it, Mr. Westcott, that's really about sixty dollars.
Mr. Westcott:	(*angrily*) Trying to be a funny one, are you? Well, I'm calling the police. I'm going to have you Drakes arrested for... for... careless use of magic pots!

(*He runs out the door.*)

Mr. Drake:	(*waving his arms at the pot*) Quit, pot, quit! Halt! Cease! That's enough, little pot! BE DONE WITH THE PORRIDGE!
Narrator:	Just then, Mrs. Drake walks in.
Mrs. Drake:	(*loudly*) STOP, POT, STOP!
Narrator:	At once, the pot stops making porridge.
Mrs. Drake:	(*frustrated*) I was gone for forty-five minutes, and just look at this place!
Brian:	(*whispering*) She was gone for about 50 minutes, Father.

(*Mr. Drake shakes his head and looks at Brian with a half-smile.*)

Mr. Drake:	Well, Brian, I think you've got it down now. (*He looks around and sighs.*) So ... about how long do you think the cleanup will take?

 THE END

Fluency Practice Read-Aloud Plays: Grades 3–4   Scholastic Teaching Resources

The Selfish Girl

❈ Adapted from a Native American Tlingit Tale ❈

CHARACTERS

Narrator 1
Narrator 2
Warrior's Mother
Warrior
Warrior's Wife

Narrator 1: A young warrior brought his wife and his mother to live along the coast of what is now known as Alaska. They made a home for themselves and hoped to find plenty of fish and wild game to eat.

Narrator 2: The summer was not fruitful, however. The fish stayed away from the shore, so the warrior couldn't catch any. He couldn't hunt, either, as deer, moose, and other animals had moved away from the coast and up to the mountains. The warrior was forced to gather meager berries and roots to feed his family.

Warrior's Mother: (*speaking to her son by the water's edge*) My son, you and I grow weaker by the day. Without food, we have no energy or strength.

(*The mother turns and looks back toward the campfire, where the warrior's wife hums and tends the fire.*)

Warrior's Mother: We are withering, but look at your wife. She is as young and healthy as the day you married her. How can that be, when none of us has any food?

Fluency Practice Read-Aloud Plays: Grades 3–4   Scholastic Teaching Resources

Warrior:	(*studying his wife from a distance*) I have wondered the same thing myself. I don't understand it.
Narrator 1:	That night, the warrior's mother tossed and turned in her sleep. She was so hungry she could almost smell fresh fish cooking over the fire.
Warrior's Mother:	(*sitting up*) I'm sure I am dreaming, but the smell is so strong that I have to see where it comes from.

(*She walks to the campfire, where she finds her son's wife huddled by the flames, eating fish and tossing the bones into the fire.*)

Warrior's Mother:	What are you doing at this hour of night, and where did you get this fish?
Warrior's Wife:	Get away, woman! You are dreaming!
Warrior's Mother:	(*reaching for a piece of fish*) I am not dreaming! I see and smell fish right in front of me! I beg you to share what you have, for I am starving!
Warrior's Wife:	I say again, you are dreaming! Go back to sleep!
Warrior's Mother:	Just a morsel, I beg you! Just a taste of the fish!
Warrior's Wife:	(*Standing up, she puts the last piece of fish in her mouth, grasps the woman's hands roughly, and speaks harshly.*) GET AWAY FROM ME, OLD WOMAN!
Narrator 2:	The next morning, the warrior's mother spoke to her son alone.
Warrior's Mother:	Well, I know the answer to why your wife is healthy while you and I fail. The answer is horrible and cruel.
Warrior:	What do you mean?

Warrior's Mother: (*Sitting down, she sadly begins to tell her story.*) Last night, I fell asleep, feeling hungry as usual. I thought I was dreaming the smell of fish cooking, so I walked to the fire and found your wife there, eating her fill of cooked salmon.

Warrior: Surely, you must have been dreaming.

Warrior's Mother: (*shaking her head*) No, I was not. I went to your wife and saw her chewing on fish, eating and eating as if she would never stop. I tapped her on the shoulder and asked that she share, that I might have some of the fish. I begged her, but she would give me none. She spoke to me harshly and ate all the fish herself.

Warrior: How can this be? Are you sure this was not just a dream?

Warrior's Mother: (*holding out her hands to show burn marks*) Your wife pressed burning hot fish bones into my hands as she pushed me away. See for yourself the burn marks on my hands.

Warrior: (*Taking his mother's hands into his own, he hangs his head.*) I am sorry for this. I am sorry that anyone I've loved would treat such a kind person badly. (*He clenches his teeth.*) Say nothing to my wife and tonight I will see for myself what she has been doing.

Warrior's Wife: (*coming up to her husband and embracing him*) Good morning, my warrior. How did you sleep last night?

Warrior: As always. (*He watches as his wife walks away and cheerfully gathers twigs for another fire.*)

Narrator 1: All day and night, the warrior watched his wife closely. That night, he lay awake when his wife thought he was asleep.

Warrior's Wife: (*to herself*) Everyone is asleep and it is time to get myself some food!

(*She stands and walks down to the shore. Unseen by his wife, the warrior rises and sneaks down to the water to watch.*)

Warrior's Wife: (*Standing knee-deep in the water, she raises her arms and sings.*) Fish of the sea! Fish of the sea! Hear my words, and come to me!

Narrator 2:   Instantly, two large salmon leaped from the water and into her arms.

Warrior's Wife: (*laughing with delight*) Oh what a delicious feast you will make, and all for me!

Narrator 1:   While the wife cooked the fish, the husband slipped back into bed and pretended to be asleep. In the morning, he went out hunting by himself. To his surprise, he caught a large seal, which he and his mother cooked at once.

Warrior's Mother: Food at last! How good this food tastes! How long we have waited!

Warrior: (*looking at his wife*) Eat more; you must be starving.

Warrior's Wife: (*filling her mouth with food*) Yes, yes. It's been so long.

Narrator 2:   Wanting to please her husband, the warrior's wife ate and ate, even though she was still feeling full from her own meal of fish. She fell soundly asleep after dinner. While she slept, the warrior went down to the water with a large basket and waded in up to his waist.

Warrior: (*raising his hands and singing*) Fish of the sea! Fish of the sea! Hear my words and come to me!

Fluency Practice Read-Aloud Plays: Grades 3–4 • Scholastic Teaching Resources

(The warrior holds out a basket, and fish jump in until the basket is full.)

Narrator 1: The next morning, the young wife awoke to the smell of fish cooking. Nervously, she rushed to the fire.

Warrior's Wife: *(staring at her husband and his mother, who are eating a feast of fish)* What's going on? The fish have come back, then?

Warrior: *(giving his wife a look of disappointment and anger)* As you know, my selfish wife, they were here all along.

Warrior's Wife: *(nervously putting a hand to her head)* I . . . I don't know what you're talking about. *(She turns and runs off into the woods.)*

Narrator 2: Knowing her selfishness was discovered, the warrior's wife ran as fast as she could toward the mountains, afraid that her husband's anger might harm her. As she climbed the mountain, she felt her body growing smaller and smaller.

Warrior's Wife: *(gasping)* What is happening to me? I am shrinking and feathers are growing from my body!

Narrator 1: Running up the mountain, the warrior saw his wife turn into an owl. She flew up and rested on the branch of a tree.

Warrior: *(staring sadly at the owl)* I was coming to forgive you and to teach you to be kind and unselfish. But I see that your selfishness has turned the magic against you. I cannot transform you, for this is the price you must pay for your selfishness.

Narrator 2: And with that, the warrior turned his back on the owl and went back to tell his mother the news. To this day, the hoot of an owl can be heard in the woods of Alaska, serving as a gentle reminder of the price a young woman once paid for her selfishness.

 THE END

CHARACTERS

Rick Terscale
Andreas Fault
Mag Nitude
Moe Shun
Shay King

Rick: Hello, and welcome to the most rockin' game show around: Earthquake! I'm your host, Rick Terscale. Let's meet today's contestants, shall we?

Andreas: I'm Andreas Fault, and I'm a restaurant manager from Cantwell, Alaska.

Mag: I'm Mag Nitude, and I'm a computer expert from Glen Rock, New Jersey.

Moe: My name is Moe Shun, and I'm a geologist at California State University.

Shay: I'm Shay King, and I run a science camp in Twin Falls, Idaho.

Rick: Okay, contestants, get ready for your first question. For 100 points, please hit your buzzers if you know the answer to: WHAT IS AN EARTHQUAKE?

(Each player hits a buzzer, but only Andreas's buzzer lights up.)

Rick: Okay, Andreas. Please tell us: WHAT IS AN EARTHQUAKE?

Fluency Practice Read-Aloud Plays: Grades 3–4 • Scholastic Teaching Resources

Andreas:	An earthquake is a shaking of the ground that can cause dishes to rattle, buildings to fall, and roads to crack and split apart.
Rick:	You're right! Our next question, for 100 points is: WHAT CAUSES AN EARTHQUAKE?

(*Mag's buzzer lights up.*)

Mag:	The earth is held up by four elephants that stand on the back of a turtle.
Moe, Shay, and Andreas:	WHAT?
Mag:	The elephants stand on the turtle, and the turtle stands on top of a cobra, which isn't easy. Have you ever tried to stand and keep your balance on a snake? When any of the animals move, the earth shakes.
Moe:	That's not science, it's legend. It's a way people used to explain earthquakes long ago, before scientists found out what really caused them.
Mag:	Man, I've believed that my whole life. What really does cause an earthquake, then?
Rick:	Contestants, please tell me: WHAT CAUSES AN EARTHQUAKE?

(*Shay's buzzer lights up.*)

Shay:	Inside the earth, there are huge slabs of rock called plates. Sometimes a plate slides out of place suddenly and pushes against another plate. When this happens, pressure builds up and causes an explosion inside the earth. The explosion makes the ground shake and sometimes crack.

Rick: Correct! The next question, for 200 points is: HOW LONG DOES AN EARTHQUAKE LAST?

(*Moe's buzzer lights up.*)

Moe: There is no set time. An earthquake might last only seconds or it might go on for one minute or more.

Rick: Right! Next question, again for 200: HOW DO SCIENTISTS COMPARE ONE EARTHQUAKE TO ANOTHER?

(*Andreas's buzzer lights up.*)

Andreas: Scientists use tools to detect the earth's motion. The more motion a quake causes, the worse the damage. What I mean is, earthquakes that cause the earth to shake a lot create more damage to the ground, buildings, and roads than earthquakes that cause only gentle vibrations.

Rick: That's right, Andreas!

Moe: (*raising his hand*) I'd like to add to that if I may, Rick.

Mag: (*staring at Moe*) You can't speak out in a game show, Moe. You have to wait until Rick asks a question.

Moe: I'm not looking for points, Mag. I just want to add something to what Andreas said.

Andreas: (*insulted*) I just got 200 points for what I said. I think it was good enough.

Moe: Well, you didn't say anything about the Richter Scale.

Andreas: I wasn't asked about the Richter Scale. I'm just here to answer the questions.

Fluency Practice Read-Aloud Plays: Grades 3–4 • Scholastic Teaching Resources

Rick: (*getting nervous*) Be calm, everyone, and we'll get to it! Now, on to my next question...

(*Mag and Andreas glare at Moe as all four contestants get ready to press their buzzers.*)

Rick: For 500 points: WHAT IS THE RICHTER SCALE?

(*Moe's buzzer lights up.*)

Mag, Andreas, and Shay: Well, that's not fair! Of course he's going to get the answer! He gave you the idea!

Moe: (*ignoring them*) For 500 points, Rick, the Richter scale is one of the measurements scientists use to tell how strong an earthquake was. People won't even feel an earthquake that measures 2 or less on the Richter scale. An earthquake that measures 8 or higher, though, causes the ground to shake violently and crack apart, causing enormous damage.

Shay: (*raising her hand*) I'd like to add something. Let's say we talk about which earthquakes happen most often in a year: ones you can feel or ones you can't feel?

Rick: (*looking through his note cards, nervously*) I don't see that question on my cards, Shay.

Shay: (*smacks her buzzer*) For 1,000 points, I say that the earthquakes that happen most often are those you can't feel—the ones that score 2 or under on the Richter scale. More than 600,000 of these happen every year, while fewer than 20 earthquakes per year score 7 or higher on the Richter Scale.

(*Andreas's buzzer lights up.*)

| Andreas: | For 5,000 points, I'd like to add this. Can earthquakes be predicted or prevented? The answer is no. Scientists know what causes earthquakes, but they can't tell when one is coming or where it's going to be. |

(*Moe's buzzer lights up.*)

| Moe: | For 10,000 points, I'd like to be more specific! Scientists can't prevent or predict earthquakes, but they can tell where on the earth quakes are most likely to happen. Places where the earth's crust is already cracked, especially places where earthquakes have already happened, are the most likely places for quakes to occur. |

(*At this point, all of the contestants frantically press their buttons, wanting to speak next.*)

| Rick: | Contestants, get hold of yourselves! This is a game show! I ask the questions! I award the points! I AM THE HOST! |

(*Mag, Moe, Shay, and Andreas leave their buttons and get out of their seats, facing each other and arguing.*)

| Rick: | (*Alarmed, he looks at the audience.*) Well, folks, that seems to be it for today. Tune in tomorrow for another unsteady episode of Earthquake! |

 THE END

Fluency Practice Read-Aloud Plays: Grades 3–4   Scholastic Teaching Resources